why❓ why❓ why❓

Which animals have scaly skin?

Clare Oliver

p

This is a Parragon Book
First published in 2001

Parragon
Queen Street House
4 Queen Street
Bath BA1 1HE, UK

Copyright © Parragon 2001

Produced by

David West 👫 Children's Books
7 Princeton Court
55 Felsham Road
Putney
London SW15 1AZ

All rights reserved. No part of this publication may be reproduced, stored in a retrieval system, or transmitted by any means, electronic, mechanical, photocopying, recording or otherwise, without the prior permission of the copyright holder.

British Library Cataloguing-in-Publication Data

A catalogue record for this book is available from the British Library.

ISBN 0-75255-361-5

Printed in Italy

Designers
Axis Design, Aarti Parmar, Rob Shone, Fiona Thorne

Illustrators
Ross Watton, Mike Taylor (SGA)

Cartoonist
Peter Wilks (SGA)

Editor
James Pickering

CONTENTS

4 What do a mosquito and an elephant have in common?

4 Which plant is really an animal?

5 What are the simplest life-forms?

6 Which animals are spineless?

6 Which is the biggest boneless creature?

7 Do worms have a skeleton?

8 What sort of animal is a lobster?

8 Who wears armour at the bottom of the sea?

9 How do crabs grow bigger?

10 Which animals have a skeleton on the outside?

10 Are spiders insects?

11 Can insects fly?

12 How do fish breathe?

12 How do salmon leap?

13 Which fish would fit on your fingertip?

14 Why are frogs slimy?

14 How can you tell a frog from a toad?

15 Which is the weirdest amphibian?

16 Which animals have scaly skin?

16 How long do tortoises live?

17 How can you tell a crocodile from an alligator?

18 Why do birds have feathers?

19 Can all birds swim?

19 Why do eagles have such hooked beaks?

20 Which animals have fur?

20 Are all mammals soft to touch?

21 Which is the tiniest mammal?

22 What type of animal is a koala?

22 Which mammal lays eggs?

23 Do all mammals breathe through the mouth?

24 Which lizard looks like a tree trunk?

24 Why are zebras stripy?

25 Who wears two fur coats?

26 Do turtles lay eggs in the sea?

26 Which bird lays the biggest egg?

27 Do tree frogs lay eggs in trees?

28 Which dad has babies?

29 Which baby bounces along?

30 How well do sharks smell?

30 Why do rabbits have big ears?

31 How do eagles find their prey?

32 Index

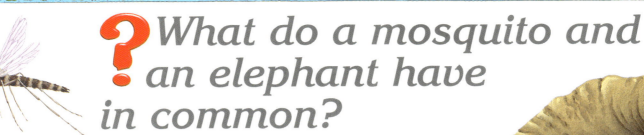

❓ What do a mosquito and an elephant have in common?

Although they are very different in shape and size, a mosquito and an elephant have something in common. They are both animals! Animals are living, breathing things that can move around to find food, shelter or a mate.

Sea cucumber

❓ Which plant is really an animal?

Despite their name sea cucumbers are animals, not plants. Their shape and knobbly skin make them look a bit like a cucumber. But unlike cucumber plants, they can move around.

❓ What are the simplest life-forms?

Protozoa are tiny life-forms, which don't have muscles like animals, but aren't plants or fungi either.

Protozoa

TRUE OR FALSE?

The only life-forms on Earth are animals.

FALSE. Plants and fungi are alive. We know this because they grow and reproduce to make copies of themselves.

All animals need sunshine.

FALSE. At the bottom of the deepest ocean, where it is cold and totally dark, there are tubeworms and other strange creatures.

❓ Which animals are spineless?

About 90 per cent of all the animals on Earth have no backbone, or spine. They are called invertebrates and range from snails to big, wobbly jellyfish. All invertebrates are cold-blooded – their body temperature is the same as the air or water around them.

Jellyfish

Giant squid

❓ Which is the biggest boneless creature?

The biggest invertebrate is the giant squid, with an 8 m-long body and even longer tentacles. It lives in the ocean, where the water supports its weight.

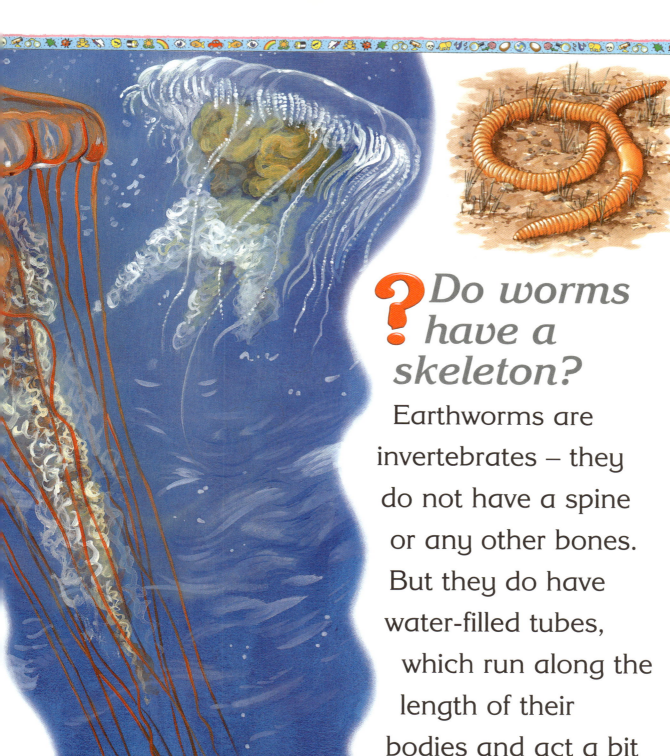

? Do worms have a skeleton?

Earthworms are invertebrates – they do not have a spine or any other bones. But they do have water-filled tubes, which run along the length of their bodies and act a bit like a skeleton.

TRUE OR FALSE?

Snails and oysters are closely related.

TRUE. Oysters and snails have soft bodies and shells. They both belong to a family of animals known as molluscs.

Starfish have five arms.

FALSE. Most do, but some have as many as 50! The arms are called 'rays', because they spread out like rays from the Sun.

What sort of animal is a lobster?

The lobster is a type of invertebrate called a crustacean. Crustaceans have shells (crusts) and lots of jointed legs. A lobster has five pairs of legs, with claws on its front ones to grip and stab prey.

Who wears armour at the bottom of the sea?

The tough outer shell of a lobster or crab is like a suit of armour, stopping hungry fish and other predators from biting the animal's body. Most crabs live on the seabed, eating rotting remains that sink down there.

Lobster

❓ How do crabs grow bigger?

Our skin stretches as we grow, but a hard shell can't stretch. When a crab grows too big for its shell, it gets rid of it. The new shell underneath is soft at first, but soon hardens. A crab may do this as many as 20 times in its life.

Crab losing shell

TRUE OR FALSE?

Crustaceans can only live in the water.

FALSE. Most crustaceans live in or around water, but land crabs and woodlice live on land. Even so, they prefer to live in damp places.

Some crabs steal shells.

TRUE. Hermit crabs don't grow their own shells. They find an old empty shell and hide their long, soft body in there instead!

Stag beetle

❓ Which animals have a skeleton on the outside?

The tough casing that protects a beetle's body is called an exoskeleton. A crab's shell is a type of exoskeleton, too. Most invertebrates rely on an outside skeleton to protect their boneless body.

❓ Are spiders insects?

Spiders aren't insects, because they have too many legs and too few body parts! An insect has six legs and three parts to its body (head, thorax and abdomen). A spider has eight legs and its head and thorax are joined.

Tarantula spider

Dragonfly

❓ Can insects fly?

The ones with wings can! Butterflies, bees and midges are flying insects that have two pairs of wings. Houseflies make do with a single pair. Some insects called termites break off their wings on purpose, when they don't need them anymore.

TRUE OR FALSE?

Centipedes have 100 feet.

FALSE. 'Centipede' means 100 feet, but some centipedes have more than 350 feet! All the better for chasing after prey!

Scorpions are closely related to spiders.

TRUE. If you count a scorpion's walking legs, you'll soon see the family resemblance. Both spiders and scorpions have eight.

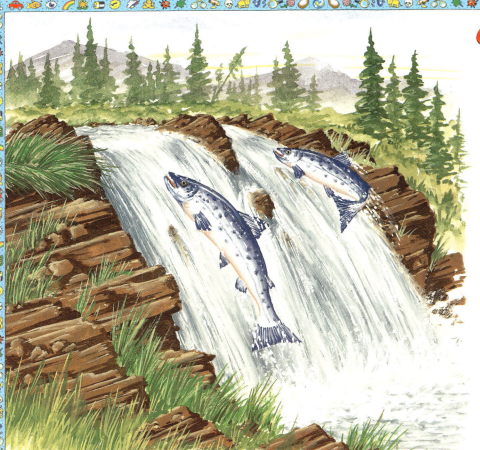

How do fish breathe?

Fish have slits called gills on the sides of their heads, that allow them to get oxygen from water, just as we get oxygen from air. All fish breathe using gills.

How do salmon leap?

Salmon leap if they meet a mini waterfall when they are heading up-river to breed. The strong, muscly tails that they use for swimming also help to thrust them up into the air.

Hammerhead shark

Dwarf goby

? Which fish would fit on your fingertip?

The dwarf goby is the tiniest fish in the world, at about 1 cm long. The whale shark is biggest – it's about 12 m long from nose to tail, but quite harmless to people.

TRUE OR FALSE?

Whales are a type of fish.

FALSE. Whales and dolphins are warm-blooded mammals, which come up for air. Fish are cold-blooded and breathe underwater.

Oarfish are as long as an oar.

FALSE. Unless it was a giant's boat! Oarfish are as long as four canoes in a row.

❓ Why are frogs slimy?

A frog's thin, slimy skin allows it to absorb oxygen from both air and water. Frogs are amphibians, animals that start life in water, but gradually change so they can survive on land, too.

Frog

Toad

❓ How can you tell a frog from a toad?

Most frogs have smooth skin, but toads are warty! Frogs and toads are the only amphibians that lose their tail and grow strong back legs for jumping.

❓ Which is the weirdest amphibian?

The axolotl never really grows up! It breeds when it is still at 'tadpole' stage and only changes into an adult body if its pond dries up and it is forced to live on land.

Axolotl

TRUE OR FALSE?

If you kiss a frog, it will magically turn into a prince.

FALSE. It's not a good idea to kiss frogs or toads, because some of them ooze poison.

The goliath frog is the biggest amphibian.

FALSE. The goliath is as long as a ruler, and the biggest frog, but the Chinese giant salamander is nearly four times as long.

❓ Which animals have scaly skin?

Snakes, lizards, crocodiles and turtles have dry, scaly skin. These cold-blooded creatures belong to a family of animals called reptiles. There are about 6,000 types of reptile.

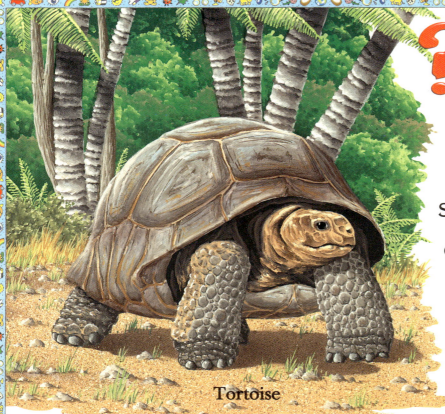

Tortoise

❓ How long do tortoises live?

Tortoises are the longest-living animals on Earth. Some probably live beyond their 200th birthday! Perhaps it's because their tough, bony shell protects them from dangerous predators.

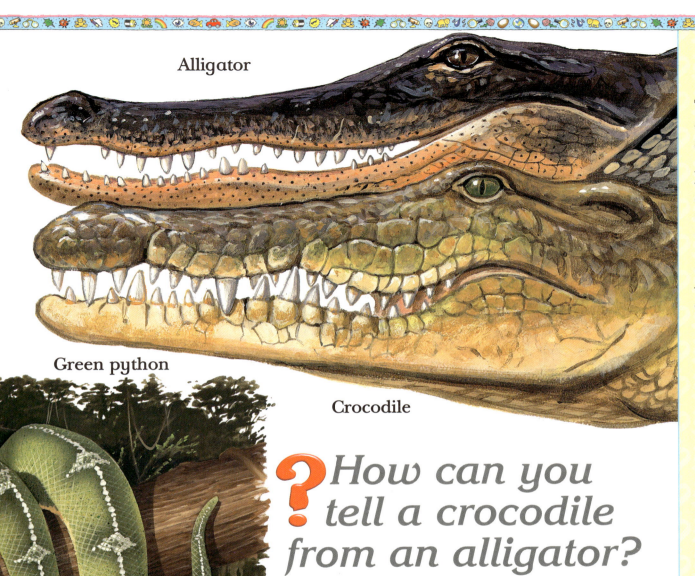

Alligator

Green python

Crocodile

❓ How can you tell a crocodile from an alligator?

You can tell them apart by their smile. When a crocodile's mouth is shut, you can still see one of its bottom teeth poking out.

TRUE OR FALSE?

Thread snakes are the longest snakes by far.

FALSE. Thread snakes are the shortest snakes at about 10 cm. Pythons are the longest – they can grow to 10 m!

Snakes aren't able to blink.

TRUE. They can't blink, because they don't have any eyelids! A see-through scale protects each of their eyes.

❓ Why do birds have feathers?

Soft, downy feathers keep birds' bodies toasty and warm, while waxy outer ones keep off the rain. Most importantly, feathers allow birds to fly. Birds beat their feathered wings to lift off the ground and fly through the air.

Parrots

❓ Can all birds swim?

Penguins

No, but some can. Penguins have webbed feet, stubby wings, oily waterproof feathers, and a layer of fat to keep them warm.

❓ Why do eagles have such hooked beaks?

Bald eagle

An eagle's hooked beak is perfect for tearing up meat. Herons have long beaks for spearing fish. Macaws have powerful beaks for cracking nuts.

TRUE OR FALSE?

All birds fly.

FALSE. Not all birds need to fly! Penguins swim instead, while ostriches, emus, rheas and kiwis all run away from their enemies.

Birds can't fly backwards.

FALSE. Hummingbirds are the only birds which fly backwards. It helps them to hover around a flower filled with nectar.

❓ Which animals have fur?

Bear and cubs

Animals that have fur are called mammals. The other things that mammals have in common are having a backbone, breathing air, being warm-blooded and feeding their babies on milk. The mammal family includes bears and monkeys, bats and mice.

❓ Are all mammals soft to touch?

Not the spiny porcupine! Although it is related to rats and mice and does have fur, the porcupine also has lots of spiky quills to protect it from its enemies.

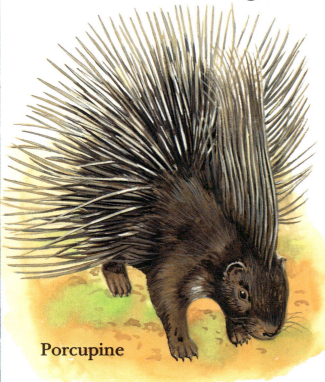
Porcupine

Bumblebee bat

❓ **Which is the tiniest mammal?**

The smallest mammal is the bumblebee bat that lives in caves in Thailand. The bat's body is only about 3 cm long. Its wingspan is much longer – about 14 cm!

TRUE OR FALSE?

All mammals live on land.

FALSE. Manatees, seals and whales live in water. They have flippers and tails, not arms and legs.

Humans are mammals.

TRUE. Hair is a type of fur, and we feed our babies on milk. Humans are primates, like chimps and gorillas.

What type of animal is a koala?

Along with kangaroos, koalas belong to a group of mammals called marsupials. Tiny baby koalas live in their mother's pouch, where they can feed on her milk for the first seven months of their life.

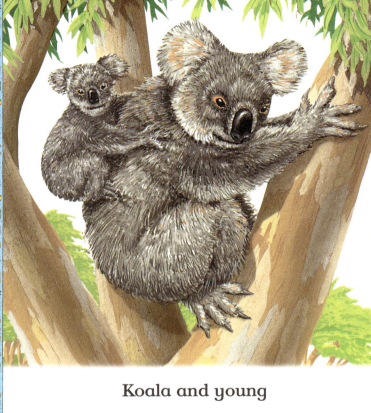

Koala and young

Which mammal lays eggs?

Unlike most mammals, the duckbilled platypus lays eggs that hatch after about ten days. The mother feeds her babies on milk, until they are big enough to hunt for fish.

Duckbilled platypus

Humpback whale

❓ Do all mammals breathe through the mouth?

No – whales breathe through a blowhole on the top of their head. When they surface, warm breath pushes out. Out in the cold, it makes a misty spout that can be as high as 12 m!

TRUE OR FALSE?

Marsupials only live in Australia.

FALSE. Koalas, wombats, possums and kangaroos live in Australia. Opossums live in North and South America.

Only two types of mammal can lay eggs.

TRUE. The platypus and echidna lay eggs. Echidna mums keep their eggs in their pouch, where the babies hatch and drink milk.

❓ Which lizard looks like a tree trunk?

The leaf-tailed gecko's speckled skin blends in perfectly with the trunk of a tree. So long as this reptile keeps still, its clever camouflage stops any predator from noticing it.

Gecko

Zebras

❓ Why are zebras stripy?

Black and white stripes confuse lions and other predators. The stripes seem to wobble in the heat haze. Each zebra has its own pattern, so stripes might also help foals find their mum in the herd.

Who wears two fur coats?

Some mammals change their coat to match the season, including the hares, foxes and wolves of the snowy north. Their brown coat turns white in winter for camouflage against the snow. It also grows extra-thick to keep out the cold.

Arctic fox

Arctic hares

TRUE OR FALSE?

Young zebra foals are black and white.

FALSE. The foal's stripes start out brown. They darken as the zebra grows. Finally they turn black.

Butterflies have eyes on their wings.

TRUE. Not for seeing with, but spots that look like huge eyes, to scare off predators.

Ostrich

❓ Do turtles lay eggs in the sea?

Turtles spend all their lives out at sea, but the mums come ashore to lay their leathery eggs. When the eggs hatch, the baby turtles crawl out of the sand and head straight down to the water.

❓ Which bird lays the biggest egg?

The biggest bird lays the biggest egg! An ostrich is much taller than an adult human, and its eggs are giant, too. A single ostrich egg weighs more than 22 chicken eggs!

❓ Do tree frogs lay eggs in trees?

Tree frog

Baby turtles

Like all frogs, tiny tree frogs need to lay their eggs in water. They use pools of rainwater cupped in the leaves of rainforest trees. There's fresh rain every day, so there's little danger of the eggs drying out.

TRUE OR FALSE?

Some fish keep their eggs in their mouths.

TRUE. Eggs left alone to hatch are often eaten by other animals. Cichlids keep their eggs safe and sound in their mouths.

The smallest bird egg of all is less than 1 cm in length.

TRUE. The egg of the vervain hummingbird is tiny – about the same size as a pea!

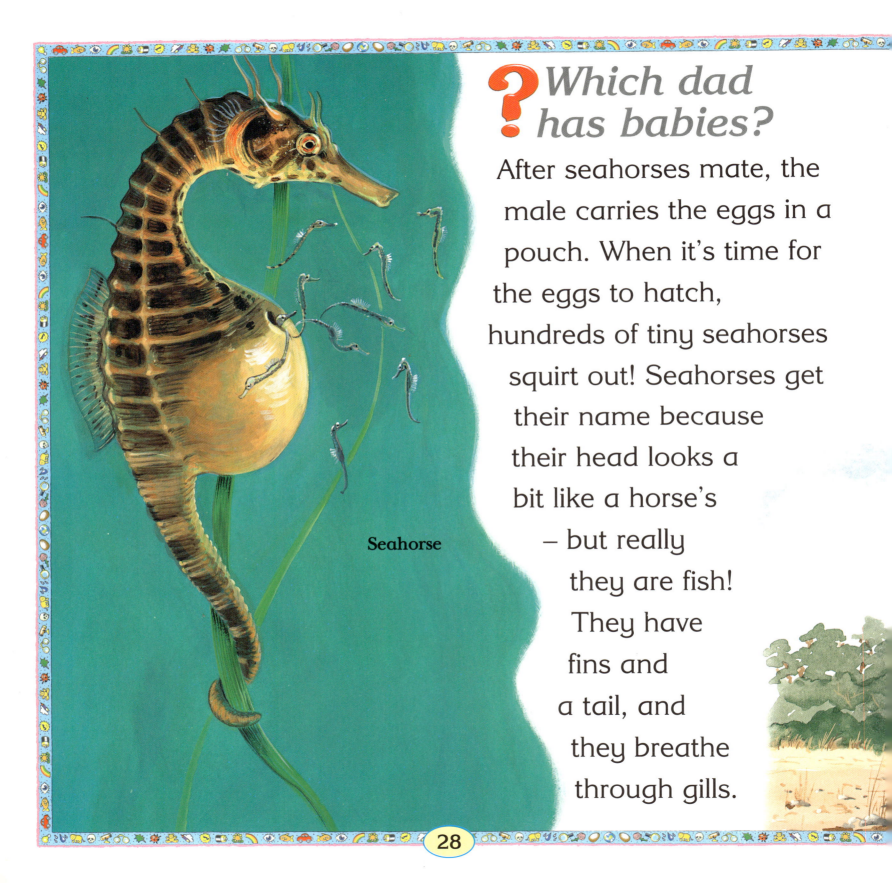

Seahorse

❓ Which dad has babies?

After seahorses mate, the male carries the eggs in a pouch. When it's time for the eggs to hatch, hundreds of tiny seahorses squirt out! Seahorses get their name because their head looks a bit like a horse's – but really they are fish! They have fins and a tail, and they breathe through gills.

❓ Which baby bounces along?

A baby kangaroo, or joey, has a very bouncy ride in its mum's pouch as she hops around. The joey is only about 2 cm long when it is born. It crawls up through its mum's fur into her pouch and stays there, drinking her milk. The joey only leaves the cosy pouch when it is about nine months old.

Kangaroo

TRUE OR FALSE?

Butterflies can fly the minute they hatch.

FALSE. Butterfly eggs hatch into hungry caterpillars. They only change into their adult form later.

Cuckoos are the best mums in the world.

FALSE. Cuckoos lay their eggs in another bird's nest, and let it keep the egg warm and feed the chick!

How well do sharks smell?

Sharks smell very well! As a shark swims, water flows in and out of its nose. If the shark picks up the scent of blood it makes a beeline for it, 'sniffing' hard to stay on course.

Great White shark

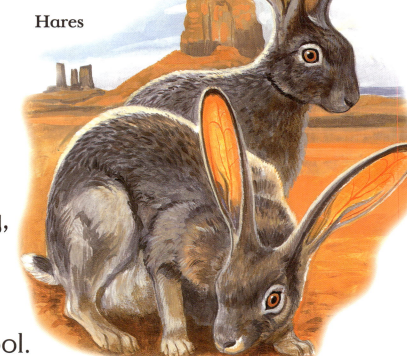
Hares

Why do rabbits have big ears?

Rabbits and hares have enormous ears for their size – and super hearing. The twitchy, outsize ears funnel the sound. Big ears also allow heat to escape, so the animals stay cool.

❓ How do eagles find their prey?

By sight – like all birds of prey, eagles have keen eyesight. A golden eagle can spot a rabbit's slightest movement on the ground from 2 km away!

Golden eagle

TRUE OR FALSE?

Ducks have see-through eyelids.

TRUE. See-through eyelids protect the ducks' eyes underwater, but still let the ducks see when they're diving for food.

Spiders aren't able to see.

FALSE. But their eyesight is bad. The jumping spider is best, but it can only see as far as the end of a ruler!

Index

alligators 17
amphibians 14–15
axolotls 15
bats 20, 21
beetles 10
birds 18, 26, 27, 29
butterflies 11, 25, 29
camouflage 24–25
crabs 8, 9, 10
crocodiles 16, 17
crustaceans 8–9
eagles 19, 31
earthworms 7
elephants 4, 5
fish 12–13, 27, 28

foxes 25
frogs 14, 15, 27
geckos 24
gobies 13
hares 25, 30
insects 10, 11
invertebrates 6–11
jellyfish 6
kangaroos 23, 29
koalas 22, 23
lobsters 8
mammals 13, 20–23, 25
molluscs 7
mosquitoes 4
ostriches 19, 26
penguins 19

platypuses 22, 23
porcupines 20
protozoa 5
rabbits 30
reptiles 16–17, 24
salmon 12
sea cucumbers 4
seahorses 28
sharks 13, 30
snakes 16, 17
spiders 10, 11, 31
squid 6
toads 14, 15
tortoises 16
turtles 16, 26
whales 13, 21, 23
zebras 24, 25